Mark Dando and Doug Ri[...] partners in 2000. They are th[...] Square, which provides speciali[...] personal and professional development for individuals, teams and organisations.

Prior to Coloured Square, Mark had experience in various HR, Management Development and coaching roles within Retail, whilst Doug gained wide UK and international experience in sales and general management positions, with organisations such as Procter & Gamble and Mattel Toys.

Mark lives in Bristol with his wife and their four children. He loves music, sport, games and cooking. Doug is married with two adult children and lives in Nottingham, with his main social activities revolving around sport and music.

They are both NLP Master Practitioners and experts in Accelerated Learning and Thinking Skills. Read more about Coloured Square at www.colouredsquare.com.

Squeeze
Your Time
■ A Mindset Book ■

Mark Dando & Doug Richardson

SilverWood

Published by the authors in 2013
using SilverWood Books Empowered Publishing ®

SilverWood Books
30 Queen Charlotte Street, Bristol, BS1 4HJ
www.silverwoodbooks.co.uk

ISBN 978-1-78132-114-0 (paperback)
ISBN 978-1-78132-177-5 (ebook)

British Library Cataloguing in Publication Data
A CIP catalogue record for this book is available from the
British Library

Set in Bembo, Trade Gothic and Frutiger by SilverWood Books
Printed on responsibly sourced paper

Squeeze Your Time

Introduction

This book is for you if you want to **be more efficient, create more space for yourself, get more done in your life, achieve more, or do more of what you want to do.**

There's nothing startling or new here.

It's not a 'time management' system book – a way to organise your diary, a set of rules and procedures to follow daily in order to organise your work.

It's a mindset book.

It provides a set of principles and ways of thinking that can transform the way you look at your time and your personal effectiveness.

We know this because it's happened to us over the last thirteen years.

To get results you'll need to **make commitments to do things differently.**

Enough...we're nearly out of time...let's get on!

Chapter One

This is a mindset book

We apologise – this first chapter is the theory chapter – what a boring way to begin! We need to get it out of the way now so that we can get down to practicalities. If you know about mindsets already, just skip it; if you don't, stick with us – we'll keep this brief.

Throughout this book, when we mention 'mindsets', we're thinking of a specific process your brain uses to filter for information.

Our senses take in a huge deluge of information every second; millions of bits of data flooding in via eyes, ears, nose etc. The brain would be overwhelmed if it actively tried to process all this information, so it doesn't. Our brains actively make decisions about what information to process and what information to filter out of our attention. As a result, the larger proportion of data received every second is discarded, or not processed by our conscious mind.

As a consequence of this we often miss large changes to our visual field, and we can fail to notice something which is right in front of our eyes – something that would be obvious to somebody else who knows it's there, knows where to look, or knows it's about to happen.

So when we mention 'mindsets' we're talking about this process by which you 'set' your mind to filter for information i.e. the largely unconscious neurological process by which your brain decides what information to pay attention to and what information to filter out or discard.

As yet, it's not very clear what it is that sets your mind in this way, but it's probably a very long list of factors: your beliefs, how you were raised, what you did yesterday, your physical state, how much alcohol you drank last night, how much exercise you've taken recently, and so on. (For more details about this topic check out the legendary work of Simons & Chabris[1], or Richard Wiseman's book, *Did You Spot the Gorilla?*[2])

One of the ways in which your mindsets may manifest themselves is in little unconscious instructions, rules or directions you give yourself – little ways in which you tell yourself to look at things... one way or another .

---

1 Daniel J Simons & Christopher Chabris, 'Gorillas in our midst: sustained inattentional blindness for dynamic events'. *Perception*, vol 28, 1999, pp1059-1074 (http://www.wjh.harvard.edu/~cfc/Simons1999.pdf)

2 Richard Wiseman, *Did You Spot the Gorilla?*, Arrow, 2004

This book will explore a few simple but significant possibilities for replacing how you look at things `one way` with how you could look at things `another` .

Chapter Two

There's no such thing as time management

Stephen R. Covey puts it really well in his book *The Seven Habits of Highly Effective People*[3], there's no such thing as time management. Time can't be managed – it just keeps going on and on whatever you do. We love this. For us there are a number of bedrock mindsets which change the way you manage your time.

Here are the first couple:

> You can't manage time   Time management doesn't exist

But, if it doesn't exist, what is left to consider in a book dedicated to time management? You know already – this isn't a book about time management at all; it's a book about self management. So, a crucial mindset to adopt is:

> Whatever time issues I have, I'm creating them somehow myself

3   Stephen R. Covey, *The Seven Habits of Highly Effective People*, Simon & Schuster Ltd, 1992, p150

We can hear you shouting at us already: "What an outrageous and stupid claim!" (Read on – you'll find more such stupid claims in the coming pages.)

You might be thinking that it's not about managing yourself at all – you might be thinking:

My boss gives me too much to do

My team creates issues that eat up my time

I just have too much to do – my role is structured in such a way that there's too much work

Yes! We know! We understand! We agree! Each of these requires a book of its own:

- "Better influencing upwards – or, how to manage my boss"

- "How to be a better team manager"

- "How to find myself a new job"

Of course, these aren't just mindsets – they're the truth – they're facts. Your boss and your team *do* cause you time management issues. Your role *may* require too much from you. But focusing on these facts won't necessarily help you to manage yourself and your time better. It may be painful, but to manage your time better, you need to set your mind to notice how:

Whatever time issues I have, I'm creating them somehow myself

And therefore:

I need to find ways to manage myself better

If you can't find it in you to accept this, then stop reading now and go find a different time management book to read – it'll save you a lot of pain.

Chapter Three

Parkinson's Law

First proposed, rather humorously, by C Northcote Parkinson in 1955, Parkinson's Law states that "work expands so as to fill the time available for its completion".[4]

We notice this principle in action a lot:

> If we have a whole list of jobs to complete and we only have Thursday left in which to complete them, we'll get them done. But, if on Thursday morning, for some reason, Friday becomes available, then it's possible we'll take Thursday and Friday to complete the same list of jobs.

> If there's a piece of work which is important to us, and we know we have to complete it today, then we'll find a way to do that – we'll make it happen somehow.

> If there's a piece of work which is important to us,

4   C Northcote Parkinson, 'Parkinson's Law', *The Economist*, Nov 19th 1955 (http://www.economist.com/node/14116121)

and we know we have to complete it by the end of next week, we'll find a way to do that.

If there's a piece of work which is important to us, and we don't have a time by which we need to complete it, it's possible we might not complete it at all.

This last one is strange, isn't it? But we come across it in the people we coach on a regular basis (and we certainly do it ourselves as well!).

If there's a piece of work which we've decided has to be completed to a particular standard, and that standard will take more time than we believe we have available, then we might not complete it until we perceive we have that time available – and that may be never!

Again – you might think this one strange, and again, we come across it in people we work with often.

Over the years, we've heard plenty of people quote Parkinson's Law, but we've never heard any of them recommend to us what to do with this idea – practically how we should apply it to ourselves and our time.

It's simple. If work expands to fill the time available, then in order to get more done you need to:

`Squeeze your time`

Stop moaning about how you need to:

`Find more time`; stop trying to: `Create more time`

Instead find ways to:

`Take time out of the diary`

`Reduce the time you have available`

There you go. We warned you we'd make further outrageous and stupid claims. There are more to come we assure you. But let's leave this one for now and come back to it later.

Chapter Four

I don't have time

Do yourself a favour – realise this is a truth. You don't have time.

There is not enough time

We hear people saying this one all the time. The problem is that we hear people say it believing that there should be enough time – believing that in some way a terrible and unique crime is being perpetrated upon them; they say it thinking that one day their workload will clear, their list of things that need to be done will shrink and there **will** be enough time.

Forget it. It's not going to happen. Probably not in a way you'll like anyway. So be careful what you wish for.

We stepped off the hamster wheel of organisational life thirteen years ago. You know that hamster wheel – the one where the organisation, your boss, your customers all conspire to give you too much work to do, in unreasonable timescales, requiring you to attend too many meetings etc.

– that hamster wheel. When we stepped off thirteen years ago we did so because we wanted to achieve more in our lives. Significantly, what we noticed, pretty quickly, was that we didn't need anybody telling us what to do, how to do it and in what timescales.

What we noticed is that we do it to ourselves! When we're in charge, we build a little hamster wheel for ourselves: slowly and carefully, over time, in ways we don't notice for a while, we put it together, and then, like a couple of silly little fluffy things, we jump on and start running.

At regular intervals we have to notice that we've constructed a little wheel for ourselves again. We have to remind ourselves:

There is not enough time

There will never be enough time

We have to know that this is a truth and start responding to it productively.

When people keep saying "I don't have time" for this or that in a lazy unthinking kind of way, we notice that they don't apply productive pressure to themselves to make things different. **If you _genuinely_ engage with the reality that** there is not enough time and there never will be, you'll have to start making choices about what you'll do and what you won't, and how long you'll give yourself to do what you'll do – so that you can make it happen.

You put yourself under productive pressure.

Chapter Five

Stop kidding yourself – you won't ever finish everything

When we talk to people about time and personal organisation, we notice that they're often working with a mindset of:

My job is to get through everything on my "to do" list or

My job is to get through everything on my "to do" list today or this week

This one's tricky. Of course this is a productive mindset – it puts pressure on us to get things done. But for some of us it makes us start earlier, or finish later…or finish much, much later…or not finish at all – work seven days a week, why not! Sadly, this kind of approach makes us less productive. With this kind of significant time available our work can expand significantly.

The negative pay-off of the mindset of "must get through everything on the list today", is that it reduces the productive pressure on us to prioritise – to make choices about what has to get done and what hasn't.

You won't finish all your work – if you can get through your task list you don't have enough to do!

Trying to get through everything encourages us to keep going with piles and piles of dross, and faffy, nit-picky, silly little jobs, when we should move on to something more important (maybe something to which we haven't attached a timescale). The time we give to faffy, silly little jobs is the time we must squeeze most aggressively, but, for some reason, this doesn't happen; it's usually the time for important non-time bound activity which gets squeezed.

So, we need to find ways to **trick ourselves** to stop doing all the silly little jobs before they take too much of our time. When we squeeze the time available for the piles of silly, faffy, nit-picky jobs, magically, without knowing how, we find ways to get them done – just not necessarily right now!

Imagine us, sitting here, in this coffee shop, writing this book right now. We don't have the time to do this! Back at our offices, the ridiculous pile of stuff to do is calling to us; it's lurking there on our shoulders, taunting us that we should be doing it now. Instead we've decided to **trick ourselves** – to sit here, drink coffee and eat fancy sandwiches in a noisy coffee shop where we can't easily use our phones, so that we can write down funny ideas that we don't know if anyone will ever read. And somehow the act of doing this – taking this 'time for stuff' out of the diary – forces us to be more decisive, more brutal with the big pile of stuff when we get back to it – tomorrow.

A quick aside – common task list traps people fall into

Realise that the use of a task list is one of those **tricks to play** on yourself that we're talking about. If you could keep all your scheduled activity in your head, and know which days you had to do it all on, you wouldn't need to use a task list at all. Your task list is just a trick you use to overcome some inefficiency in yourself.

Since it's a trick you play on yourself, make sure you keep looking for ways to increase the level of trickiness – how you're fooling yourself – otherwise it will stop working; you'll find ways to get around it.

Common traps, or ways in which you might use your task list so that its trickiness decreases:

- **Writing a task on to today's list because you received it today** – don't automatically do this – write it straight into a future day on which you'll need to get it done (unless it's got to be done immediately).

- **Leaving the list as it is through the day, even though you know you won't get through it all.** Knowing you won't get through everything today, cross some items out before you even begin, and move them to future dates – get rid of them out of your sight if they don't have to be done today. If you're good enough at this trick, you might realise you can take the afternoon off!

- **Failing to notice items which you seem to be able to move forward indefinitely** – make it your target to see how many things you can move forward so many times, that you can cross them out completely – remove them forever now that you've realised they just didn't need to be done in the first place.

- **Reading your e-mails, rather than 'processing' them on to your task list** – we've noticed a tendency in some people (including ourselves) to read through their list of e-mails, without actively deciding that "I'm doing e-mail jobs right now for twenty minutes". When they don't make this decision they can drift into looking through e-mails in an ad hoc "I've got a minute so I'll have a quick look" kind of way. In this state of 'drifting into it' we've noticed that they end up doing neither one thing nor another. They're reading e-mails, thinking "that one's too big – I don't have time for it right now – leave it 'til later". And when they do this, they're accidentally treating their in-box as another 'task list' – now they've got two task lists – very inefficient. And this is a common cause of jobs or queries that just get missed altogether.

- **Keeping the format of your task list the same** – you should notice that after a certain period of time the format stops working – your brain gets so used to it, that it stops making you think properly about what's in front of you. Muck about with the format somehow. More on this in a bit.

Chapter Six

The time you finish work for the day is random – but it matters

Since there will always be more jobs to do, since you will never get through your task list, and since your work will expand to fill the time you have available, you should know that the time at which you finish work for the day is a random time. There is no law written into our genes that we should get out on the Savannah to search for nuts and berries, or hunt animals by 9.00 a.m. and that we should stop this activity at 5.30 p.m. This is an invention and it's a fairly random one, e.g. we could easily finish at 5.00 instead! Or 4.30...4.00...3.30.

And, given Parkinson's Law, just imagine how much more work we might get through if we did.

Similarly, notice the randomness involved when you decide regularly to work on into the evening. When do you stop? "When I've done enough", is usually the answer. But how much is enough? You could work 'til two in the morning and you still wouldn't get through everything, so the time you finish is a random time – or rather it's purely your decision.

This random finish time that you've decided upon is significant. If you regularly decide that you will work on to a particular time this can become a kind of 'negative trick' you play on yourself.

Here's what we mean: we've coached many people who describe how they get caught up in meetings that they *have* to attend all the way through the day, knowing that, back at the desk, 150 e-mails are coming in, waiting to be answered, and twenty voicemails are being left, waiting to be answered. How can someone deal with this? The answer we hear quite frequently is "I stay 'til 7.30 p.m. and get all my e-mails cleared then". Of course, they also point out, quite reasonably, that after 6-ish they become much more productive anyway because people stop ringing, and there are no more meetings to go to.

This makes perfect sense – it's a very strong strategy for dealing with the madness of organisational life (even if it's just you and your mate in the organisation). On the flip side, it doesn't make any sense – in itself it is just more madness – a common piece of Groupthink that proposes this is a sensible way to deal with the situation.

When people adopt a regular strategy of working later, we notice they quickly adopt a mindset through the day of:

We've coached in very big, well known organisations in which hundreds, thousands of people are attending overly long, ineffective, not-needed-in-the-first-place meetings, at which they find out very little, and add little value – and they do this all day, most days. Then they get to their desk to do their work from 6–7.30 p.m.!

In this situation, the

It's OK...I'll get my work done from 6–7.30 p.m.

mindset is one of the things stopping people building productive pressure on themselves – the productive pressure that would mean they have to find different ways of coping (which usually involves finding ways to not attend an unproductive meeting, or at least not attend the whole meeting).

This is the same for all kinds of work patterns: weekend working, coming in early in the morning, having no lunch break, and so on. It relates directly back to Parkinson's Law and the logical conclusion that we need to squeeze our time available, rather than expand our time available.

Weekend working, coming in early and staying late – these are the working patterns that will stop you from increasing the pressure on yourself to find different, more efficient, more effective ways to cope. All of

us who do this need to wake up and realise what silly little fluffy creatures we are – what lovely little hamster wheels we've built for ourselves, and how skilful we are at running on them!

Chapter Seven

Squeeze your time – build up productive pressure on yourself

Just reading the title of this chapter might have you screaming at us. We know this one's an outrageous and unreasonable claim. But we've found on a regular basis that it's true.

If you put too much time in the diary, you'll use it. And then you'll start filling it up with too-detailed responses to e-mails and voicemails, you'll accept that you have to attend all kinds of pointless meetings, read all those cc e-mail attachments ("just to keep me in the loop"), you'll believe you must write pointless reports that nobody reads.

So, the first thing to do is to find ways to take available time out of your diary. Obviously the early mornings and late nights are an easy target. Even if you just remove one or two of these it will make an immediate difference to your levels of efficiency and effectiveness. But this isn't as easy as it sounds – as we'll explore in the next chapter, you'll need to find more elaborate ways to trick yourself.

Recently one of our team challenged a client of ours to reduce the times of her meetings by fifty per cent. He rang one of us immediately after he'd issued the challenge, for some coaching of his own – he didn't think she'd bought it as an idea. He thought he'd over-stepped the mark – that he might have gone too far. But two weeks later she rang him to explain that she'd done it, and that, as a result, all of her peer group had done it too. They still achieved as much as they ever had through their meetings (in fact they suspected they might be achieving more), and they saved a huge amount of time. They were over the moon.

Weird! How can this happen? Simple: giving themselves less time, they found ways to make their conversations more succinct, their decisions clearer etc.

Think about those weeks when you've had to attend a two-day training course, or when you've had two days annual leave. It's a mystery how you manage to still get everything done, and make everything happen (and of course, you don't). But this is just another example of the same principle in action. In this way an approaching holiday is like a trick we play on ourselves to make choices and be more productive.

Find ways to reduce your time available e.g. in contradiction to what we've said above, you could try to add **more meetings** into your schedule – **just remember, this won't work if you then stay late, arrive early or miss lunch in order to accommodate these!** For this to work you have to find ways to cope with the amount of work you've got to do **without adding any 'replacement time' into the diary.**

Warning: Stress!

Now let's consider the serious issue here. In the short term – until you find new ways of working – this approach is going to increase your stress levels. We know this to be true also, because we've done it, and we've experienced the stress. This is very dangerous – you need to be careful with it.

The whole point is to build the productive pressure on yourself – but this is about doing this consciously in order that you find new ways, different standards, alternative practices that enable you to make better decisions to get work done more efficiently. **Decreasing your time available and insisting you carry on working in exactly the same way you always have will not work. You will only increase your stress levels – it will not help you. It will make you ill.**

We don't recommend it.

Please don't do it.

Chapter Eight

Pay attention to yourself – learn what you're like – notice the traps you build for yourself

In order that you find new ways to work, so that removing time from your diary makes sense, it will help for you to pay attention to what your behavioural habits are, and therefore spot the kinds of traps that are going to be likely for you personally.

We like this very traditional four box model, intended to help us think about the kind of behaviours we each typically prefer. For a really detailed understanding we recommend you check out a full book on the topic – there are several available[5], but for our purposes here, some really basic distinctions will be enough.

Note: the basic distinctions presented in the text on four styles below isn't based on any particular source material (including the reading suggested); instead it's based on the kind of common characteristics that we've noticed as we've worked with people over the last thirteen years.

5 Robert Bolton & Dorothy Grover Bolton, *Social Style/Management Style*, Amacom, 1984 or David W Merrill & Roger H Reid, *Personal Styles & Effective Performance*, Chilton Book Company, 1981

Are you a gregarious, high energy type, who makes a noise and wants to be noticed – a Tigger-ish kind of person?

Do you find things out by connecting up with people, in preference to researching and reading by yourself?

Do you find you get things done by connecting up with other people, by finding people who can make things happen?

Do you keep picking up the phone to talk to one more person, meet for one more coffee, before getting down to work?

Are you straightforward, direct and to the point? Do you like to make things happen with little fuss?

Do you like to be presented with a summary rather than research the detail of a topic?

Are you more concerned with getting results than you are with doing things 'fully'?

Do you like to be decisive and get things moving quickly, knowing that you can of course correct later, rather than worry about getting the right decision now?

Are you a gentle, sympathetic type, who likes to care for people, find out how people are, and make sure they're all right?

Do you like to get things done, by getting on with people, and appealing to them for help and support?

Do you make things happen to avoid disappointing people or in order to please?

Do you like to check how a piece of work will affect others, whether it will cause difficulty for others, before getting it done?

Are you a cerebral, analytical type, who likes to think things through, and consider plenty of information in order to make a decision?

Do you find things out by thinking, reading, researching? Do you like detail?

Do you like to get things done by thinking them through first and considering the evidence?

Do you like to know that a piece of work has been designed properly and that it will meet the correct objective, before you get started on it, before you can finish it?

It's entirely normal for people to demonstrate a mix of one, two or three of these behavioural approaches; but it's also entirely normal to have an underlying default approach that demonstrates some typical features of one style in particular. It will be very useful for you to start to notice patterns in your behaviour, because each of these styles presents its

Do you distract yourself from getting on with jobs, by phoning, meeting and networking?

Are you absent from your desk for long periods – talking to people, networking and making connections?

Do you sometimes get bored with detail, so that you fail to put the hard work in at the right moment?

Do you rarely distract yourself from getting on with jobs – instead you're not satisfied until you get everything done?

Are you continuously checking up on what people are doing – because you can't let go of work or controls?

Are you someone who can't let go – you have to over-control and stay involved in everything (too much)? Can't be late – can't let go of uncompleted work?

own challenges to the person trying to manage him or herself. Work out which one seems to describe you best – get feedback from colleagues and peers if you need to. Let's look at some of the typical ways people with each of these behavioural styles mismanage themselves and their time.

Do you distract yourself from getting on with jobs by chatting, checking on others and dealing with requests for help?

Do you promote an 'open door' policy, welcome others' interruptions and spend too much time trying to 'help'?

Do you naturally take on too much work – can't say no?

Do you distract yourself from getting on with jobs by seeking more information or thinking things through one more time?

Do you usually want more time and reassurance that you're making the right decision?

Are you prone to keep trying to do 'just one more job' – making yourself late for appointments and meetings or personal life commitments?

Which one or two are you?

If you can work it out, then you can engage with the typical ways in which you conspire to make yourself less effective. If you can work this out, then you'll be better able to identify some basic tricks to play on yourself; so that you effectively starve yourself of your normal unproductive behaviours at the right moments.

But don't expect this to feel comfortable either. Quite the opposite, if you deliberately find ways to stop yourself doing things in your normal or habitual manner, you can expect this to feel highly unnatural, uncomfortable and even stressful (again). And this is why you need to personalise your tricks – to find ones that genuinely deal with your own habitual ways of behaving; this is why they need to be good tricks – because you won't naturally want to do this – because if you wait for it to feel comfortable, it'll never happen.

Chapter Nine

Trick yourself

To make all this work, you have to trick yourself to be different. Don't expect to be able to be different just because you think it's a good idea. If this were the case you would have made useful and effective changes some time ago – and they would have worked.

Don't expect to be able to leave the office at 5.30 or 6.00 p.m. instead of your usual 7.30 p.m. just because you've suddenly decided this would be a good idea. You'll find ways to get around it, and somehow hang around 'til your target time…because it won't feel right…or natural.

Don't expect to be able to let go of the endless detail you habitually feel you need in order to make a decision – you might feel panicked – you'll want that detail. Instead you'll have to trick yourself into coping with less time to trawl for the detail.

Don't expect to feel instantly great when you say 'no' to someone's request for help – you'll need to find some way to trick yourself that this **is** the right thing to do, and you can overcome your sense of discomfort.

The reason we need to find 'tricks' is actually *because* of the discomfort, unnaturalness (even possible panic) that we might feel as soon as we try to lessen our reliance on habitual behaviours which are causing us to take too much time, or which are causing us to mismanage ourselves. We won't naturally be able to change these behaviours **because** they can immediately *feel* 'wrong'. They're not wrong, they're just not habitual – but they can *feel* 'wrong'.

So what kind of tricks are we talking about? In the following chapters you'll find a few examples to get you going. It's not an exhaustive list by any means. You're going to need to spot your own – identifying specific things that tackle your personal habits, and you're going to need to keep coming up with new tricks to get yourself to do things that don't seem very natural or comfortable to you. Some people find this easier to do with someone else – someone who knows them well and understands the kinds of habitual behaviours involved.

Tricks to squeeze your time

- Book and pre-pay for non-cancellable activities for yourself on certain evenings of the week, which means you have to leave work earlier (and at a particular time) e.g. tickets to the theatre or a squash match. Make sure you feel they can't be cancelled either because of who you'll let down or because you've spent too much money already to make it acceptable for you to do so.

- Tell everyone you meet what time you've got to leave, and why, and who you'll let down if you don't (to your annoyance they should all keep reminding you through the day and particularly as the deadline approaches).

- Book important meetings to follow unproductive ones (so that everyone understands that you have to leave on time – no discussion).

- Instigate working patterns which allow you to turn down your attendance at some meetings altogether (e.g. we've come across plenty of people who seem to be able to turn down meetings on days when they're allowed to work from home).

- Book early morning appointments with the doctor or dentist, so that you can't get in early to compensate.

- Book and pay for one of the above early evening appointments on the same day so that this day is squeezed at both ends.

- Book the dentist for first thing in the morning on the first day back at work after a holiday. Go to a coffee shop to read through your e-mails before you get to the office (amazing how productive this one is!).

- Put time into the day to take productive breaks – i.e. a break where your brain does something entirely different (but something productive) e.g. if you're working from home take three breaks of fifteen minutes to learn a new song on the guitar or read twenty pages of a novel (again it's amazing how this one increases your productivity more than taking a break at your desk).

- Do some exercise in the middle of the day, or the middle of the afternoon (this increases your productivity in several ways at once – you squeeze your time, but you also change your state, re-oxegenate your brain etc.). *Of course some of you are reading this and saying "are you mad – as if I can leave my desk in the middle of the afternoon and go for a run round the outside of the building?!"* Well you can – you'll need a change of mindset to do it, but you can. If you look out the window right now, you might be able to see a little knot of people under a shelter in the car park outside your office – that little group that appears three or four times a day to have a quick smoke. They know what they're doing – they're squeezing their time, changing their state, having a chat and doing deep breathing exercises – and plenty of people accept that it's just something that happens. Get out there with your track shoes on! Lead yourself better!

Tricks to get down to productive work

- Book a meeting room – book a meeting – but don't invite anyone else – really – get it into your diary or your Outlook schedule. Write in names of made-up people if you need to (if that's what it takes).

- Get yourself away from your desk to work in places where you can't be disturbed e.g. coffee shops, the park on a sunny day – deliberately find places where your phone signal and Wi-Fi is poor, so that you can't use the usual bombardment of information as an excuse not to get things done.

- Unplug or switch off your phone for a time period.

- Switch off your Wi-Fi for a time period.

- Delete that computer game that you like to play, compulsively, between jobs.

- Leave your desk for a time – and leave all your faffy, nit-picky distracting jobs at the desk – only take with you that big, important piece of work that you won't get on with otherwise.

- Just decide you're on an 'away-day' today. Put an outgoing message on your e-mail that you're not available and that you won't be responding to e-mails until tomorrow.

- Do the same with your voicemail and switch off your phone.

- Turn off that annoying little pinging sound that 'pings' to let you know every time a new e-mail arrives in your in-box.

- Tape a piece of A4 paper over your monitor so that when you casually glance at your screen you can't see those e-mails arriving either!

- Wear a hat to denote that you're not available to talk at the moment (and agree with members of your team that this is the signal that you're not to be interrupted). We know teams of people who've decided on this mad approach in the past. *We don't like it ourselves – but, if it works for you, why not!*

Tricks to preserve productive time in the diary

- Find the thing which, when it's written in your diary, stays written there. For Mark this is 'holiday', for Doug this is 'golf'. Notice what you write in your diary that often gets de-prioritised the moment something important comes along. For example in our diary 'office', 'admin', 'design meeting', are diary entries that often get de-prioritised when something important comes along. So for Mark, sometimes he has to write 'holiday' in his diary, when it's just a day when he wants to do something important (like write this book). It's stupid – he even knows he's playing this trick on himself – but he also knows that if he writes 'book-writing' then this has a tendency to get de-prioritised in favour of paid coaching or training work. Sometimes only 'holiday' will ensure this time remains available in the diary.

- Book and pay for a particular venue for an activity that you want to ensure happens – in preference to all the usual nit-picky, dross jobs e.g. pay for a meeting room, at a specific venue, one hour's drive away from work. Somehow this one always works, to ensure that we don't give this time away to someone else, for something else (again it's pathetic but it works).

Keep noticing tricks that other people play on themselves, to help them manage themselves. Here's one we're not recommending, but which is a great example.

People who smoke, trick themselves to get all kinds of things that others of us don't. People who smoke don't think twice about taking a break halfway through a meeting, to go outside, breathe deeply, take a 'time out' from the discussion points of the meeting, maybe have a chat to other people smoking, maybe just have some time to think by themselves. When we're coaching we meet plenty of people who would love to take these kinds of Time Outs to do these deep breathing exercises, have some time to themselves and reflect for a short while on what's been discussed so far. But they tell us they don't know how to do it; bizarrely without the excuse of smoking they have mindsets like:

I'm not allowed to   That would be rude

People won't understand

But it's entirely possible to come up with tricks that allow you to give yourself permission to enforce this kind of discipline if you want to. Just make sure that, as you join the meeting, you make it clear that:

- You've got two or three vital phone calls that you will have to take at various intervals

- You have to get back to your desk at a certain time to issue some instructions to the team

- You're going to need to get something to drink, or eat, in a while

- You have to go to another meeting half way through this one

- Maybe you've even got a weak bladder and you'll need to nip to the loo a few times.

Now all this might strike you as lying and you might not approve. Great point! Remember the important thing here is to find things which trick YOU – you're not trying to lie to people, you're trying to find ways to manage YOURSELF better. If this is too much like lying for you, or if it just strikes you as too silly and convoluted, don't do it – you need to find particular tricks or prompts for yourself that work to give you permission to manage yourself differently. Maybe you can't be bothered with this 'trick' thing for something as straightforward as this, and you just need to start informing people that you're going to take a break from your meeting every thirty minutes for a breath of fresh air and to reflect on what's been discussed – just be refreshingly different and straightforward about it!

Chapter Ten

Keep tricking yourself – don't let up – you're too skilful – you'll find ways around your own tricks

To implement this kind of change successfully you'll need to trick yourself. Then you'll need to trick yourself again. Then you'll need to re-invent your tricks – you're too skilful – you'll find ways to start getting around your own tricks.

Your diary is a major and primary example of this. We've said it before – the diary is just a big elaborate trick to play on yourself, designed to make you more productive, more effective and efficient.

Look at the various pages in your diary. Check out the way they're designed – essentially they provide you with a bunch of prompts to direct your thinking, and direct the way you think about your time, your tasks and the way you organise your work. What we notice is that some people are using the same diary page they've used for the last ten years (some for the last thirty years). **Now, if this is working for you, then please don't change** anything – we meet plenty of people who know exactly how to use the same system they've always used to manage their thinking and behaviours to get done everything they want to get done – and to do it really effectively. If you're someone like this, we don't recommend you consider changing anything.

If you're not someone like this, if you notice all kinds of ways in which you'd like to get more productive, then notice the ways in which your diary no longer works. Also notice the ways in which the prompts in your diary no longer make you think about what work to do, how long to do it for, and in what order.

We redesign our diary pages on a regular basis to re-arrange the prompts, group information differently, give ourselves reminders of how we should be thinking and so on. We colour-code different information so that it stands out in particular ways, slaps us in the face and so on.

Take your task list as a really simple example – think about how you could redesign this, so that information is grouped together differently e.g. all e-mail jobs listed together, all phone jobs listed together.

Try drawing ten boxes on your page and giving each one a different header – then logging the relevant work under each header.

And so on.

We don't really know what you need to do for yourself – the key principle here is just to recognise that if the tricks you're playing on yourself stop working, you need to invent new tricks – with the diary this might just mean changing the way it looks or the way it's laid out.

The key mindset with the tricks you play on yourself is:

If it's not working, change something – anything! Find a new trick that does work.

Chapter Eleven

Manage your state

This is a big one. There's a whole book needed on this one (and not enough time to do it here, of course!). So we're just going to start you thinking about a few simple principles here.

Your ability to manage yourself effectively relies on you being in a resourceful state – when you're ridiculously stressed, tangled up, overly rushed etc. you're not very resourceful, and you're going to find it difficult to respond well to situations.

So your ability to cope with and manage yourself, AND your ability to cope with increasing the productive pressure on yourself relies on you keeping yourself in a productive state throughout.

To do this, we propose that you get clear about the critical success factors that drive a resourceful state in you. And these critical success factors drive personal KPIs (Key Performance Indicators) – activities or ways of doing stuff, which, if you deliver on them, *indicate* that your performance is on track (in this case indicating that your personal resourcefulness is on track).

This is a relatively simple process, but one that requires some focused time and thinking, on a regular basis, to identify the things that really make the difference, as follows:

Critical Success Factors for me to remain resourceful	My Minimum Standards (I believe this is the minimum required to deliver my Critical Success Factors)
To stay fit and feel fit enough	▪ Run thirty minutes once per week ▪ Seven to eight hours sleep, five days per week ▪ No alcohol on week days ▪ Short break every six weeks ▪ Four pints of water per day

Again these are just examples – and you might think they're quite demanding, or not demanding enough. Critical success factors and the minimum standards attached are very personal and should be different for different people. They require you to notice what's really important to you. For a few different examples check out what a number of our clients have described to us on the following pages.

Client A

Critical Success Factors for me to remain resourceful	My Minimum Standards (I believe this is the minimum required to deliver my Critical Success Factors)
Get personal down-time when I'm not in over-drive thinking about work.	■ Hairdressers once per week (she didn't need her hair done this often – it was just the only place and time where she was trapped in one place with nothing work-like to think about – she'd read *Hello!*). ■ Do my grocery shopping before 5 p.m. on Friday (she explained that after working mad hours all week she wanted to ensure that weekends were all hers – therefore she wanted to make sure that the supermarket was no longer the first thing she did in her personal time as she began the weekend).

Client B

Feeling I have a strong base at home – staying well connected with my family.	■ Walk the kids to school once per week. ■ Home for breakfast once per week. ■ Home in time for dinner once per week. ■ No TV – just talk to my partner – once per week.

Client C

Time for me.	■ Go to a coffee shop by myself (read the paper) for two hours – once per month.

Client D

Feed my brain – feel like I'm developing and growing.	■ Read two random pages of a business book – twice a week. ■ Finish one book per month.

These things are really important – if you can't keep yourself in a resourceful state, it will be very difficult for you to apply any of the other principles in this short book. It's absolutely at the heart of good self management (time management if you still think of it this way). So, we recommend you begin to notice what it is that really keeps you in a resourceful state, and the actions you need to take (no matter how individualistic and strange to others) that will deliver that resourceful state for you.

Chapter Twelve

Keep it going – it's a never ending job

This is a never ending process – it doesn't stop – there's always plenty more to learn about the way to apply these principles; as we write these words, we're embarking on another re-invention of our way of working – right now we're applying the principles to ourselves with renewed vigour in order to get more of what we want, in order to achieve more in our lives, in order that we can complete more!

And we think this is kind of the point with self management – it's a never ending project; it takes work – unless, of course, you get to a point at which you're completely happy.

We are constantly redoubling our efforts to apply the mindsets and principles we've outlined above, so that we can squeeze our time more or differently, to get more of what we want.

So don't expect that once you've implemented these

principles you're done. You'll have only just begun.

And that's enough for now – time's up!

Find out more about Coloured Square at
www.colouredsquare.com

Lightning Source UK Ltd.
Milton Keynes UK
UKIC03n1603150316
270203UK00002B/6